CW00349399

★ **Aardman** presents

The Joy of Shaun

Embrace Love with Shaun the Sheep

First published 2003 by Boxtree
an imprint of Pan Macmillan Ltd
Pan Macmillan, 20 New Wharf Road, London N1 9RR
Basingstoke and Oxford
Associated companies throughout the world
www.panmacmillan.com

ISBN 0 7522 1557 4

Produced under license by Aardman Animations © and ™ Aardman/Wallace and Gromit Ltd 2003

Text © Pan Macmillan Ltd 2003

2 4 6 8 9 7 5 3

A CIP catalogue record for this book is available from the British Library.

Design by Dan Newman @ Perfect Bound Ltd
Text by Annie Schafheitle and Natalie Jerome

Printed by Proost, Belgium

★ **Aardman** presents

The Joy of Shaun

Embrace Love with Shaun the Sheep

B■XTREE

You're just too good to be true

Shaun finds eye contact
is crucial in attracting
a partner.

YOU MAY SEE A STRANGER

Cupid can strike
at the unlikeliest of times.

*K*NOWING ME, KNOWING YOU

Shaun is the only relationship expert you will ever need.

*H*OLD IT BABY

'*Stop in the* N*ame of* L*ove*'
is G*romit's favourite*
love song.

Breaking up is hard to do . . .
so wash that ewe
right out of your hair!

A NIGHT TO REMEMBER

It's important to look your best, but in matters of the heart it's personality that counts.

WHEN A RAM LOVES A WOMAN

*Shaun demonstrates the art of
being single and fabulous.*

WALKING ON SUNSHINE

When you really love someone, distance is no object — Wallace would go to the ends of the earth for Wendolene.

*Curb any jealous tendencies,
or you could end up in
the dog house.*

YOU WERE ALWAYS ON MY MIND...

Playing 'your song' can help to mend a broken heart.

Just singin' in the rain...

Gromit makes sure
he is prepared for his
moonlight serenade.

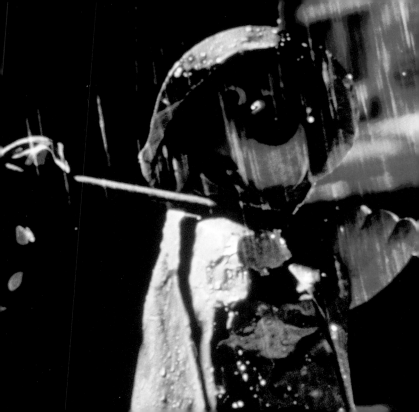

STAND BY YOUR MAN

If you love someone, you support them in the good times… and the bad.

THE FIRST CUT IS THE DEEPEST

*If only there was
a plaster for a
broken heart.*

Y OU CAN LEAVE YOUR HAT ON

There are always lessons to learn in love. Make sure you have a good teacher!

YOU DRIVE ME CRAZY

Remember there's
a thin line between
love and hate.

WHAT A WAY TO MAKE A LIVIN'

Working late can play havoc in any relationship. Set aside quality time to be with each other.

$\mathcal{L}$OVE SHINE A LIGHT

Press the right buttons
and you'll find someone
to love you for life.

TWO'S COMPANY

Monogamy is often an underrated quality in a relationship.

He's a cheesy lover

Cheese is a little-known but highly effective aphrodisiac – according to Wallace.

I HOPE LIFE TREATS YOU KIND

Remember there are always
more fish in the sea.

*A portrait of yourself
can be a touching gift
for a loved one.*